TURNING POINTS

THE EXTREME CLIMATE

BY MICHAEL E. GOODMAN

CREATIVE EDUCATION • CREATIVE PAPERBACKS

Published by Creative Education and Creative Paperbacks
P.O. Box 227, Mankato, Minnesota 56002
Creative Education and Creative Paperbacks are imprints of
The Creative Company
www.thecreativecompany.us

Design by The Design Lab
Production by Colin O'Dea
Art direction by Rita Marshall
Printed in China

Photographs by BigStock (ronstik), Creative Commons Wikimedia (Jacob
Freeze/Flickr, Antti Lipponen/Flickr, NASA Expedition 20 crew/NASA
Earth Observatory, Sergey Pesterev), Getty Images (ISAAC KASAMANI/
AFP, NurPhoto, Liz Pedersen/EyeEm, Anton Petrus/Moment, Issarawat
Tattong/Moment), iStockphoto (35007, AndrewJalbert, CatLane, dmelnikau,
FilippoBacci, Jan-Otto, Dominic Jeanmaire, lisatop, Pgiam, SeppFriedhuber,
stevecoleimages, taviphoto, Yelantsevv), National Geographic Creative
(AARON HUEY, JOE SCHERSCHEL)

Library of Congress Cataloging-in-Publication Data

Names: Goodman, Michael E., author.
Title: The extreme climate / Michael E. Goodman.
Series: Turning points.
Includes bibliographical references and index.
Summary: A historical account of extreme weather events and climate patterns,
including human events leading up to observable changes, the people involved
in studying trends, and the lingering aftermath.
Identifiers: ISBN 978-1-64026-179-2 (hardcover) / ISBN 978-1-62832-742-7
(pbk) / ISBN 978-1-64000-297-5 (eBook)
This title has been submitted for CIP processing under LCCN 2019935248.

CCSS: RI.5.1, 2, 3, 8; RI. 6.1, 2, 4, 7; RH.6–8.3, 4, 5, 6, 7, 8

First Edition HC 9 8 7 6 5 4 3 2 1
First Edition PBK 9 8 7 6 5 4 3 2 1

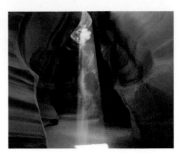

TABLE *of* CONTENTS

On October 19, 2012, weather forecasters at the National Hurricane Center in Miami, Florida, noticed a storm gathering in the eastern Atlantic Ocean off the coast of Africa. At first, it was known as "Tropical Depression 18," or the 18th storm of the season. Its wind speed kept increasing as it moved across the Atlantic. On October 22, it was officially named Tropical Storm Sandy, the 18th name on that year's alphabetical list. By October 24, the wind speeds reached **hurricane level**, and the storm became Hurricane Sandy.

At first, Sandy acted like a normal hurricane. It was energized by the warm waters of the Caribbean and tracked northward as it moved toward the United States. Some forecasters hopefully predicted that it would turn east and head harmlessly out into the North Atlantic. But Sandy suddenly changed direction on October 28 and began heading west, directly toward New Jersey, and into one of the country's most populous regions. No storm had made such a dramatic turn in 160 years. Meteorologists gave the huge storm a new name—"Superstorm Sandy"—and urged those living along the coast to evacuate inland.

Over the next 10 days, Superstorm Sandy plunged much of the metropolitan New York area into darkness and caused more than $70 billion in damages. Weather scientists began analyzing what had caused Sandy to act the way it did. They also theorized about how changes in Earth's **climate** might lead to more superstorms and other extreme weather events in the future.

Eons of geological and climatic changes
have shaped the planet we call home, but
human activities have also accelerated
the pace and magnitude of those changes.

Weather stations are scattered throughout the world, from remote mountains in Finland (pictured) to the coastlines of Australia.

CHAPTER ONE

TRACKING TRENDS

Most people start their day by checking the weather. Is it hot, cold, mild, wet, dry, windy, or calm outside? Knowing the weather helps people decide everything from what to wear to what activities to plan—whether to go outside or stay inside. Earth has weather because it is surrounded by a blanket of gases called the atmosphere. The blanket extends about 600 miles (966 km) above and around the surface of Earth. It provides a filter from the sun's heat that protects the planet from hot or cold temperature extremes that would otherwise make most life impossible. The lowest layer of the atmosphere, about six miles (9.7 km) up, is called the troposphere. The troposphere is our weather headquarters. It is filled with swirling gases and **water vapor**, some of which are heated to form clouds. As the clouds become denser and heavier, they release some of the water as rain or snow. Differences in air pressure within the troposphere also result in winds of various speeds that move the clouds.

Anemometer

To work, barometers depend upon air pressure and vacuums—both of which Torricelli had to prove existed, because the concepts ran contrary to accepted science of the day.

People have been studying and predicting weather for thousands of years. The Greek philosopher Aristotle (384–322 B.C.) coined the word *meteorology*, a term that we still use today, to name the science of weather. Many years later, **Renaissance** scientists developed instruments to measure different elements of weather. In 1593, Italian mathematician Galileo Galilei invented a prototype thermometer used to measure air temperature. His assistant, Evangelista Torricelli, later invented the first barometer to measure air pressure. Galileo's device was never very accurate; German physicist Daniel Gabriel Fahrenheit improved the tool in 1714. Other instruments were soon designed to measure humidity, or moisture in the air. Scientists recognized the need to consider conditions such as temperature, air pressure, and humidity in order to describe and predict weather.

Today's meteorologists use sophisticated tools on land, at sea, and in the air to monitor and forecast the weather. A United Nations (UN) agency called the World Meteorological Organization oversees 11,000 fixed weather stations constructed in countries around the world. These stations send out reports every three hours to a group of regional weather centers. The centers then pass on the data to local areas. There are also more than 1,200 weather stations located on buoys that float freely with ocean currents and send readings back to land via satellites. All these devices keep track of temperature and air pressure changes, wind speeds and direction, cloud movements, storm fronts, and precipitation (rainfall and snowfall). In addition, weather balloons, planes, and satellites take and transmit photographs that show weather conditions from the air.

While meteorology has been an area of study for a long time, *climatology*—the study of climate history and change—is a much newer subject. Weather and climate are closely related, but they have different meanings. Weather consists of short-term changes in the atmosphere—as observed hourly or daily. Climate, on the other hand, explains how the weather behaves over relatively long periods, such as decades or centuries. On its website, the National Aeronautics and Space Administration (NASA) explains an easy way to remember the difference between climate and weather: Climate is what you expect over a period of time, such as a hot and wet summer, and weather is what you get at the moment, such as a steamy day with a sudden thunderstorm. Climatologists usually look at averages in monthly temperature ranges or precipitation over a 30-year period to develop their analyses.

Climatologists first began focusing on climate issues in the mid-1800s. They studied how land areas, oceans, polar ice masses, and

Thanks to crews aboard the International Space Station, Earth's weather and cloud patterns can even be observed from just outside the atmosphere.

AMERICA'S DEADLIEST HURRICANE

*On September 8, 1900, a hurricane accompanied by a 16-foot (4.9 m) **storm surge** struck at Galveston, Texas, on the Gulf of Mexico. Nearly 20 percent of the city's population of 37,000 died in flooding caused by the storm. It is still ranked as the deadliest hurricane in U.S. history. Galveston was totally unprepared for the storm. When the hurricane was passing over Cuba, the Weather Bureau, based in Washington, predicted it would move north and east. When the storm turned west, it was too late to warn Galveston residents of the danger coming their way. The 1900 hurricane convinced weather experts to develop a better warning system to help keep people safe.*

winds absorb heat from the sun and move the heat around. They also began observing and collecting data to determine if Earth's climate is changing. They noted that our world has been warming measurably since around 1900. They analyzed the data to determine how this global warming might be affecting the formation and movement of storms and resulting in extreme weather conditions such as heat waves, floods, and **droughts**.

Nearly all climatologists today believe Earth's climate is undergoing significant changes—most of which are negative. The National Oceanic and Atmospheric Administration (NOAA), a division of NASA that focuses on the conditions of the oceans and the atmosphere, has provided the following findings as evidence for this position:

- Earth's average surface temperature has been on the rise since the late 19th century. To measure surface temperature, scientists use readings made by weather stations and buoys of the air above land and ocean surfaces. Then they compare the current readings to those made at intervals in the past. The amount of increase has varied from decade to decade since 1890, but there has been a consistent upward movement. The readings show that most of the warming has occurred in the past 35 years, with the 5 warmest years on record taking place since 2010.

- The oceans have absorbed much of this increased heat, with the top 700 meters (2,297 ft) of ocean warming more than 0.4 °F (.22 °C) since 1969.

- Polar ice sheets in Greenland and Antarctica have decreased in size significantly as air and water temperatures have increased and are melting at an increased rate each decade.

- Global **sea level** rose about eight inches (20.3 cm) in the last century, and has been rising more quickly since 2000. Part of the sea level rise is a result of polar ice melting.

- The number of high-temperature days per year has been increasing. The number of heavy rainfall events per year has also been going up.

Climatologists are worried about current trends, and they have published several alarming reports in recent years. One report issued in October 2018 by the UN's Intergovernmental Panel on Climate Change (IPCC) warned that countries must take steps before the year 2030 to keep the rate of global warming down. If not, several catastrophic events might happen. For example, increased global warming could lead to more extremely hot days every summer, which could result in more heat-related deaths and more devastating forest fires. Higher temperatures would also mean more melting of polar ice that could further raise sea levels and flood coastal areas—where much of the world's population lives. A higher rate of global warming could also destroy land and coastal habitats for many animals, ranging from tiny insects that help pollinate crops to huge polar bears.

The IPCC report urged governments to work together to slow global warming by reducing the use of **fossil fuels** and suggested actions that individuals could take. For instance, those who own homes could better insulate the structures,

Extreme weather conditions such as flash floods can, over time, have a beautiful effect on canyons and other geological formations.

Though apex predators, polar bears are also dependent on human behaviors, which are contributing to warming trends that decrease the availability of sea ice.

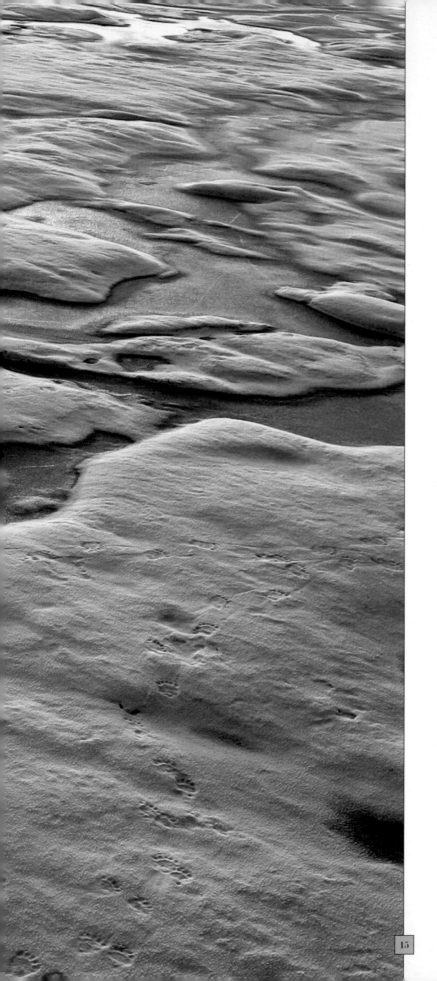

especially around attics, doors, and windows. This could reduce the consumption of energy from fossil fuels. Another energy-saving idea is to install more **solar panels** to generate renewable energy. A third idea involves changing how we get around: Rather than contributing more vehicles to the roads, people could take public transportation where available and walk and cycle more often. Methods for mitigating the effects of warming and adapting to different lifestyles, the report concluded, are within our grasp.

POINTING OUT

SAME STORM, DIFFERENT NAME

Hurricanes, typhoons, and cyclones are all storms with powerful swirling winds and heavy rains. In fact, they are different names for the same kind of extreme storm. Hurricanes occur in the Atlantic Ocean and the northeast Pacific. The origin of the word hurricane *is "Hurakan," a Mayan god known for causing strong winds. During a voyage in 1502, Christopher Columbus first experienced a hurricane. The word* typhoon *is based on an Arabic word meaning "whirlwind." Typhoons occur in the northern and western Pacific. Cyclones, or "circling storms," occur in the South Pacific and Indian Oceans. Meteorologists use the term "tropical cyclones" to refer to all three storms.*

CHAPTER TWO

EARTH'S GREENHOUSE

Most people agree that Earth's climate is warming. However, not everyone agrees that people are the major cause of climate change. To better understand the issue, it is important to understand just how people and nature interact today and how that relationship is changing the climate.

There was climate on Earth long before people came on the scene. There was also climate change. There were periods of extreme cold in which **glaciers** covered the land and oceans froze solid. There were also long periods of thawing. Animal and plant life grew and changed during the thawing periods. It is estimated that human life began about 200,000 years ago. Those first humans often faced harsh weather but somehow survived. Earth scientists believe that we are in a thawing period now, known as the Holocene, which started about 12,000 years ago. Some scientists refer to the Holocene as the "age of people" because the human population on Earth has grown so rapidly during this time—from about 5 million to approximately 7 billion.

One main reason that humans have flourished during the Holocene is that temperatures have been fairly warm and steady throughout the period. Earth is heated naturally by a process known as the "greenhouse effect." Light from the sun enters Earth's atmosphere and warms the ground and oceans,

Freezing and thawing phenomena can be witnessed on a much smaller scale in wintry lakes: as surface temperatures increase, ice coverage lasts for shorter periods.

17

much as light enters a greenhouse and warms plants inside. Some of the sun's heat bounces back in the form of infrared rays. These rays are kept from escaping back into space when they are absorbed by gases in the atmosphere, especially carbon dioxide (CO_2). The greenhouse effect involves a delicate balance. Climatologists worry that human activity, particularly in the past 250 years, may be destroying that balance.

What has been significantly different about climate change in the distant past and climate change recently is the **industrialization** that began in the 1700s. To generate power to run machines in factories and homes, to propel vehicles, or to heat and cool buildings, people

POINTING OUT

SKELETONS ON ICE

*In 1942, a park ranger in India spotted the bones of several hundred people underwater in a mountain lake. Local people believed the bones were the skeletons of soldiers who had died in battle during a war. Eventually, some of the bones were brought up from the lake and tested to see how old the skeletons were and what might have caused the men's deaths. As it turned out, the bones were more than 1,100 years old. Testing also showed that the people were probably struck on the head by hard, round balls of ice during one of the deadliest **hailstorms** in history.*

An overabundance of emissions can interfere with the natural processes of circulating carbon by photosynthesis and respiration (the inhaling of oxygen and exhaling of carbon dioxide).

began burning more and more fossil fuels, such as coal, oil, and gas. One byproduct of fossil fuel burning is an increase of CO_2 in the atmosphere. Some CO_2 is vital. Without enough heat-trapping CO_2, Earth's temperature would be too cold to sustain human life. With too much CO_2, however, our atmosphere might overheat. That seems to be going on today. Based on measurements that climatologists have been taking since around 1850, Earth has gotten about 1.3 °F (.72 °C) warmer on average. And the average temperature increase is expected to go up even faster in the future. If the temperature in your home goes up less than a degree, you may not notice the change very much. However, if the whole planet heats up even a small amount, there can be major consequences for all life forms.

That is what meteorologists thought was happening in 1988. It was a turning point for weather scientists. In 1988, U.S. weather did not follow normal climate patterns. Spring temperatures were above normal, summer temperatures were sweltering, and fall temperatures remained extremely high. In May, record high temperatures were recorded in 13 American cities. In June, another 69 American cities set heat records. In July, the temperature in normally moderate San Francisco hit 103 °F (39 °C). Los Angeles topped that record with a 110 °F (43 °C) reading in September. People were not the only ones suffering. Farmers in North Carolina reported that the severe heat wave resulted in the deaths of 166,000 chickens and 15,000 turkeys.

The weather was not only hot in 1988, but it was also very dry. The Midwest experienced one of the worst droughts ever. Without rain, crops withered, and farmland dried up. The water level in rivers and lakes also fell. It was inevitable that heat and dryness would lead to fires breaking out. That is what happened in Yellowstone National Park, where 36 percent of the trees and other vegetation were destroyed by fire in the summer of 1988.

U.S. government leaders wondered if all these weather events could be interrelated. A senate committee invited James Hansen, director of NASA's Goddard Institute for Space Studies, to explain what was happening. Hansen presented studies that linked the record heat and drought to the greenhouse effect and to human activity. He urged leaders in the U.S. and around the world to begin taking steps as soon as possible to deal with climate change. Hansen's remarks helped prompt the UN to form the IPCC. The panel has been assessing scientific studies related to climate change ever since, publishing reports on the findings every five years.

While Hansen focused his attention on the impact of global warming on land, other NASA scientists looked for connections between global warming and storm activities taking place over Earth's oceans. They noted that readings from buoys and satellites showed that surface temperatures of ocean waters have been increasing since the 1970s. So has the temperature of air above the oceans. Because warm air holds more water vapor than cold air, rising air temperatures have led to an increase in the amount of water vapor in the atmosphere. Warmer oceans and warmer air above the oceans result in

From 2015 through 2018, California experienced 10 of its 20 most destructive—in terms of structures destroyed—wildfires on record.

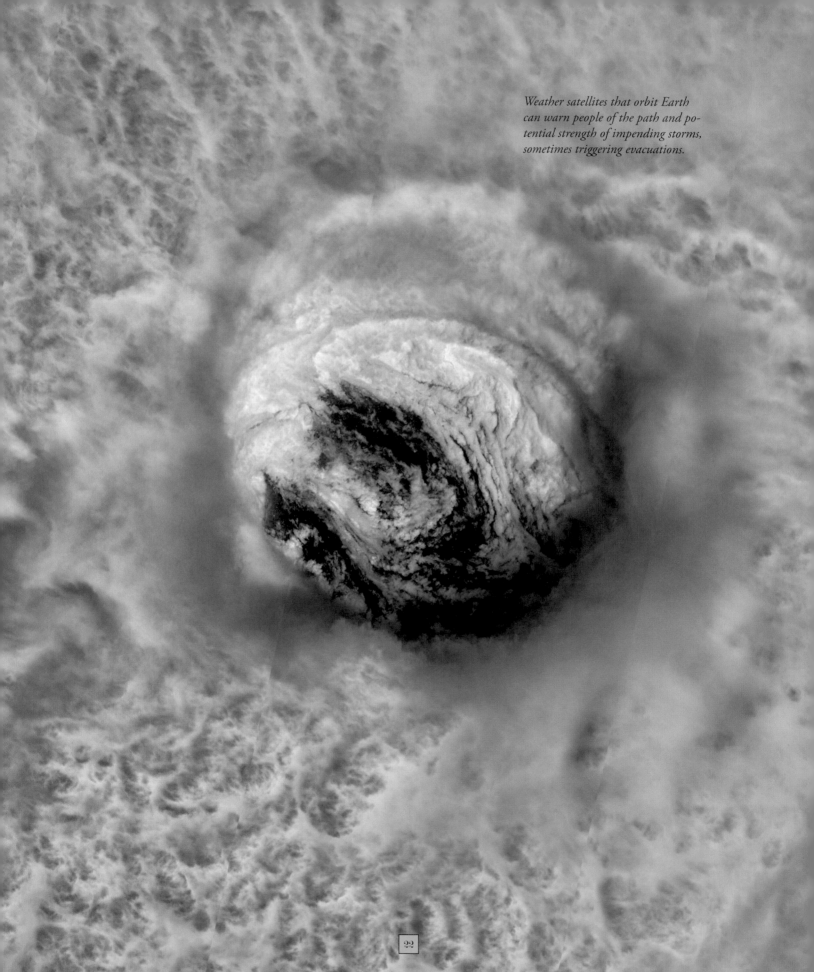

Weather satellites that orbit Earth can warn people of the path and potential strength of impending storms, sometimes triggering evacuations.

a perfect "breeding ground" for severe storms such as hurricanes. These storms require high humidity, strong winds, and surface ocean temperatures that exceed 79 °F (26 °C). The rising of warm, moist air from the ocean combines with water vapor already in the atmosphere to feed the storm. So, it might seem logical that global warming has led to an increase in the number and intensity of hurricanes. Recent statistics seem to support this conclusion.

Between 1969 and 1999, in the North Atlantic Basin (an area encompassing the Caribbean and parts of North America), there were an average of 11 named tropical storms each year. A named tropical storm is promoted to hurricane level when its winds reach 74 miles (119 km) per hour. Approximately 6 of those 11 reached hurricane level each of those years. More recently, from 2000 to 2013, the average has been around 16 named tropical storms per year, with approximately 8 becoming hurricanes. Most scientists think this increase is related, at least in part, to global warming. They also believe that the combination of warmer waters and warmer air above those waters has been leading to larger, stronger, and longer-lasting storms.

A number of these devastating storms made **landfall** in the U.S. in the 2000s. Hurricane Katrina, which struck the Gulf Coast near New Orleans in 2005, is one of the deadliest and most costly hurricanes in American history. More than 1,800 people died as a result of Katrina.

POINTING OUT

NAMES AND NO NAMES

Since 1953, Atlantic hurricanes have been given names from alphabetical lists compiled by the National Hurricane Center in Miami, Florida. One name is assigned each year for 21 letters (all except q, u, x, y, and z). The names are supposed to be recycled after six years. So the names used in 2019 may be reused in 2025. However, the names of some especially deadly or costly storms have been retired forever, such as Camille, Hugo, Katrina, Sandy, Matthew, Harvey, and Maria. They will be replaced on the list by other names. Different lists are used to name typhoons and cyclones.

Damages from the storm were estimated at $160 billion. Parts of the New York and New Jersey coast were still recovering from the impact of 2012's Superstorm Sandy years later. Slow-moving Hurricane Harvey drenched the Houston, Texas, area with more than 60 inches (152 cm) of rain over a 4-day period in August 2017. And Hurricane Maria destroyed much of the island of Puerto Rico in September 2017.

CHAPTER THREE

GOING TO EXTREMES

Think about the weather events you or your family members have experienced in your lives. Have you ever been drenched or buffeted by a hurricane or taken shelter from a tornado? What is the hottest day you have sweated through or the coldest day you have shivered through? The most consecutive days of rain or the longest period of drought? The most violent thunderstorm? The most frightening lightning strikes? All of these come under the heading of "extreme weather events."

Hurricanes, tornadoes, flash floods, extreme heat, wildfires, **tsunamis**, severe thunderstorms, mudslides, snow and ice storms … the list can seem pretty scary. Luckily, not every part of Earth experiences all of these extremes. There is some concern, however, that global warming may be causing extreme events to occur more frequently and with greater impact. For example, much of the planet is experiencing heat waves of greater frequency and intensity than in the past. These present a very real danger. According to a report issued by the National Weather Service (NWS), more people on average die of heat-related causes each year than as a result of hurricanes, tornadoes, floods, or lightning.

Hurricane activity is also increasing today. The increase is not so much in the number of storms but in their strength or size. Hurricanes are given

Even in dry areas such as deserts, excessive and prolonged heat can have detrimental effects on the plants and animals in that ecosystem.

a category ranking of 1 to 5, based on the strength of their sustained winds. The chart below shows characteristics of each category, as described by the Saffir-Simpson Scale. This scale was developed by wind engineer Herbert Saffir and meteorologist Robert Simpson in the 1970s as a tool for alerting the public about the possible impact of hurricanes.

Based on a NASA analysis of global hurricane data, the number of storms per year that are rated Category 2 or Category 3 has increased significantly since 1980. Storms are sustaining hurricane wind speeds for longer periods

POINTING OUT

SAFFIR-SIMPSON SCALE

Category	Sustained Wind Speeds	Typical Damage Caused
1	74–95 mph (119–153 km)	May break off tree branches and damage power lines
2	96–110 mph (154–177 km)	Can uproot smaller trees and block roads; can cause near-total power loss
3	111–130 mph (179–209 km)	May blow out windows on high-rise buildings and snap large tree branches
4	131–155 mph (211–249 km)	May collapse poorly constructed homes, break windows, and send damaging debris flying
5	>155 mph (249 km)	May cause complete collapse of some buildings; may fell a significant number of trees

While living in Florida, Herbert Saffir observed tropical-storm wind strength firsthand, informing his development of the hurricane-ranking scale.

In 1979, Hurricane David made landfall in the Dominican Republic as a Category 5 storm and was responsible for more than 2,000 deaths.

of time after they first make landfall, leading to more damage over a wider geographical range. Some of today's storms are also moving more slowly than in previous times, and there is a greater chance that they will drop record amounts of rain, as Hurricane Harvey did in 2017.

Category ranking is one way that meteorologists measure the power and destructiveness of hurricanes. But sometimes a new way is needed. That's what happened with Hurricane Sandy in 2012. Sandy began as a Category 1 storm when it entered the Caribbean region. Then its winds sped up between Jamaica and Cuba, and it was elevated to Category 2. As it traveled in the Atlantic between Florida and Virginia, Sandy was back to a Category 1. Then something unusual occurred. As Sandy was seemingly ready to head safely eastward into the Atlantic, it ran into a cold front coming down

Sandy satellite image

from Canada, which changed its wind patterns. Sandy turned to the west and began heading toward Atlantic City, New Jersey. Its winds were strengthened by the combination of storm fronts, and its overall size was expanded. It became so huge and dangerous that weather forecasters decided to call it a "Superstorm." Meteorologists believe that many more superstorms will occur in the future as a result of global warming.

Hurricanes are not the only types of extreme weather events that are intensifying in the 21st century. Perhaps the most deadly events are tsunamis, which typically occur in the Pacific or Indian Oceans. *Tsunami* is a Japanese word meaning "harbor wave." Tsunamis usually follow earthquakes that shift land and open areas along the seafloor. The ocean waters move in to fill the gap. Then the waters are pushed outward as a series of giant, fast-moving waves. The waves, which can reach speeds of nearly 500 miles (805 km) per hour, often overflow anything in their path as they hit the shore.

One of the world's most powerful tsunamis occurred the day after Christmas in 2004. It began with a major earthquake centered near Indonesia. That set off giant waves that rushed

POINTING OUT

BOILED BATS AND FROZEN IGUANAS

Extreme changes in climate are affecting many animal species. In southeastern Australia, where temperatures in 2018 reached more than 110 °F (43.3 °C), several hundred large bats—gray-headed flying foxes—dropped from the sky, killed by the heat. In contrast, in South Florida, where temperatures were much colder than usual, numerous iguanas fell from trees, temporarily frozen. When temperatures warmed up days later, some of the iguanas recovered. Sharks in the waters near Cape Cod in Massachusetts were not as lucky as the iguanas. After a severe cold front called a "bomb cyclone" struck in March 2018, many thresher sharks washed up on the beach, frozen to death.

Seaside communities must contend with many natural variables, including huge waves that have the potential to achieve tsunami strength.

ashore throughout southern Asia. In all, 230,000 people in 14 different countries died as a result. The tsunami became one of the deadliest natural disasters ever recorded.

Extreme weather is not something new, though. The world has been experiencing extreme weather events for hundreds of years. Some we know about; others were probably never written or talked about. Here are a few of the most memorable weather events of the past:

- On May 19, 1780, most of New England experienced nighttime darkness in the middle of the day. Many religious New Englanders believed that the world was ending. The cause of the darkness was later determined to be heavy cloud cover combined with thick smoke from nearby forest fires.

- The year 1816 became known as the "Year Without a Summer." Temperatures stayed far below normal all summer long throughout the U.S., Canada, and Western Europe. A heavy snow fell in New England in June. Many parts of the world— including China and India—experienced extreme rains and droughts, and farmers worldwide lost most of their crops. What had caused the extreme summer chill? The eruption of a volcano in Indonesia in April 1815 had sent tons of ash and poisonous gases into the air, where they remained for a long time. The ash reduced the heat and light of the sun, affecting the entire Northern Hemisphere.

- Cyclones in the Bay of Bengal in northeastern India can be particularly destructive. One cyclone in October 1864 created a 40-foot (12.2 m) wall of water that flooded the entire city of Calcutta (Kolkata). More than 60,000 people were killed during the storm. Many thousands more died later from disease.

- In the Australian summer from October 1923 to April 1924, parts of Western Australia experienced a world heat-wave record of 160 consecutive days when the temperature topped 100 °F (37.8 °C).

Extreme weather has even influenced wars in history. In 1415, heavy rains and deep mud helped the British defeat the French in the decisive Battle of Agincourt during the Hundred Years' War (1337–1453). In 1588, when the ships of the **Spanish Armada** were sailing into English waters, strong winds stalled the invading ships and helped the English sink much of the Spanish fleet. A destructive hurricane in the Caribbean in 1780 sank many British ships that might have been used to fight the Continental forces during the American Revolution. Bitterly cold Russian winters also played an important role in the defeat

Caribbean shipwreck

of both Napoleon's French army in 1812 and Adolf Hitler's German army in 1942.

Weather and wind are powerful forces that act on everything from rocks and sand to the inhabitants of all types of landscapes.

CHAPTER FOUR

SURVIVAL PLANNING

Extreme weather events seem to be happening more frequently in current times. Heat waves and snowstorms, flash floods and droughts, mudslides and wildfires are constantly in the news. In the year 2018 alone, a winter storm in January brought record snowfalls as far south as Savannah, Georgia. A record heat wave struck the Northeast in February. In April and May, Minneapolis, Minnesota, went from its heaviest April snowstorm on record to a Memorial Day high of 100 °F (37.8 °C) in just six weeks' time. In June, Wyoming residents suffered through two extremely powerful tornadoes only days apart. In late June, students in Gander, Newfoundland, had to trudge through mounds of snow during their last week of school. September saw Hurricane Florence dumping huge amounts of rain on South Carolina and North Carolina. In November, years of drought combined with high winds led to massive wildfires in both northern and southern California. The entire town of Paradise, located near Sacramento, was leveled, as fire destroyed nearly 13,000 structures and killed more than 80 people.

It is quite possible that you will come face-to-face with an extreme weather event in your life. Suppose the weather forecast where you live calls for a hurricane, tornado, flooding rains, a heat wave, or a blinding

Firefighters can combat isolated structural fires with water, but containing the spread of wildfires is a much different story.

It's important to maintain a basic disaster supplies kit, replacing any expired items, so that it will be ready to go whenever needed.

EMERGENCY CANDLES

FIRST AID KIT

MATCHES

DISASTER PREPARATI

- WATER
- NON-PERISHABLE FOOD
- BATTERY RADIO
- BATTERIES
- FIRST AID KIT
- FLASHLIGHT
- BLANKET
- CANDLES
- CAN OPENER
- PRESCRIPTION MEDS
- PET FOOD

- CELL
- MAT
- WHI
- CAS
- HAN
- BAS
- TRAS
- BABY
- EMER
- PERS
- DUST

snowstorm. Would you know what to do to keep yourself and your family safe? Meteorologists and emergency management experts have both been focusing on the best ways to survive weather emergencies. Numerous books and Internet websites are available with advice. At the core of it all is the need to develop a family disaster plan and to create a personal emergency supply kit. Some good ideas are posted on the Department of Homeland Security website. The American Red Cross has also published step-by-step emergency plans.

Craig Fugate, former administrator of the Federal Emergency Management Agency

POINTING OUT

PET EMERGENCY PLAN

When people with pets are forced to evacuate their homes in a weather emergency, what should they do with their pets? Of course, it would be best to take their pets with them. However, not all shelters, hotels, or motels will accept pets. So it is important to determine before an emergency which places to go with pets or the best places to leave pets. Veterinarians recommend microchipping pets as a permanent form of identification. Owners should also carry recent pictures of their pets with them in case they become separated from the pets and need to make a "lost" poster.

(FEMA), urges people to plan ahead for emergencies. "You won't have time when severe weather hits to talk with your family and figure out what to do. It has to be done in advance, especially if you are not all together when the emergency happens," Fugate advises.

Fugate believes that it is very important to know the latest information about what is happening in your area. He suggests having a battery-powered radio that has a weather band, and replacing the batteries every six months to make sure they work. He also suggests programming emergency numbers into family members' cell phones.

The Red Cross says any family plan should have three parts: (1) Family or household members should discuss how to prepare and respond to the types of emergencies that are most likely to happen where they live, learn, work, and play. (2) They should identify responsibilities for each member of the household so that they work together as a team. (3) They should practice as many elements of the plan as possible ahead of time. The family plan should also cover what to do if members get separated. In that case, two meeting places should be chosen—one nearby and another outside the neighborhood, if it is not safe to stay near home.

A disaster supply kit can be just as vital as an emergency plan. Here are some suggestions from the Red Cross of what to include in a disaster supply kit: a three-day supply of water and nonperishable food per person; a flashlight and extra batteries; a first aid kit and manual; copies of important documents secured in a waterproof container;

Flint strike fire starter

In areas ravaged by floods, the Red Cross and other relief agencies focus on supplying clean water and other critical needs.

a whistle; cell phone chargers; extra clothing, blankets, and towels; tools such as matches (in a waterproof container), scissors, and duct tape; paper dishes and cups, plastic utensils, and plastic garbage bags.

Each type of weather disaster poses its own problems. For example, preparing for a hurricane means securing roofs and boarding up windows to prevent glass from breaking and endangering people inside the home. It is also a good idea to clear any rain gutters of debris that might clog them in a heavy rain. Also disinfect the bathtub

POINTING OUT

UNFCCC

At a conference in Paris in December 2015, most of the world's nations signed an agreement to increase use of green energy sources, reduce use of fossil fuels, and take other measures to limit global warming. The agreement is known as the United Nations Framework Convention on Climate Change (UNFCCC). The signees agreed to submit plans detailing what actions their countries would take to help meet specific global warming reduction goals. They also agreed to pledge money to help implement the pact. In 2017, president Donald Trump announced plans to withdraw from the agreement because he believed it would be too costly for the U.S. and might negatively impact American industries.

People who want their governments and other leaders to listen to concerns about climate change may take part in public demonstrations.

and fill it with water for bathing or for flushing toilets if the home water supply gets cut off.

Tornado safety calls for different preparation. First, you need to decide whether to evacuate your home and go to a public shelter or stay home and wait out the tornado. The choice may be determined by the amount of time available before the tornado hits. If you stay home, get away from windows and outside walls. Seek the lowest and most central part of the home or go into a bathroom where the walls are usually reinforced by water pipes. Try to get under a mattress or cover yourself with blankets to help protect against blowing debris. After a tornado passes, the most important thing is to check your own safety and then to see if others need help.

Flash floods are particularly dangerous, whether you are caught while riding in a car or while walking. If in a car, the best advice is to turn around and not drive through the water. It is hard to judge just how deep the water is. If the car is stuck, power down the windows before the car's electrical system shorts out. You may need to escape through a window. If you abandon the vehicle, make sure you have a clear path to higher ground. If not, it may be best to climb on the car's roof and wait for help.

In case of a heat wave, some important tips include these precautions: Avoid strenuous activity. Dress for summer in lightweight,

Emergency planning is not just for individuals or families—entire organizations and professionals are devoted to readying themselves to respond.

light-colored clothing. Cut down on protein consumption, which can increase body heat. Drink plenty of water and limit caffeinated beverages. Never leave children or pets alone inside a car, even with the windows down.

What do experts suggest doing if someone is caught in a car in a heavy snowstorm? First of all, it is best to stay put unless a building is nearby. Make sure the exhaust pipe is clear of snow, so **carbon monoxide** will not build up. Turn the car off to conserve gas, but turn it on for short periods of time to let the heater warm you up. Keep your hazard lights on, both to alert rescuers and to make sure other cars don't run into yours.

Emergency planning may become more and more important if Earth's air and waters continue to undergo warming. It is vital that government leaders around the world focus on how best to deal with climate change and how best to help people prepare for extreme weather events. The turning point is now.

10,000 B.C.	The Holocene Epoch, or "the age of people," begins.
A.D. **1593**	Galileo Galilei invents an early thermometer to measure air temperature.
1644	Evangelista Torricelli invents a mercury barometer to measure air pressure.
1714	Daniel Fahrenheit invents a mercury thermometer that measures air temperature more accurately than Galileo's.
1769	James Watt patents an improved steam engine that is considered the starting point of the Industrial Revolution.
1780	The Great Hurricane of 1780 kills more than 20,000 in the Caribbean and sinks many British ships sailing to the battlefields of the American Revolution.
1815	Indonesia's Mount Tambora volcano erupts, affecting weather patterns throughout the Northern Hemisphere for more than a year.
1864	Most of Kolkata, India, is destroyed by a powerful cyclone and tidal wave.
1900	The deadliest hurricane in U.S. history strikes Galveston, Texas, on the Gulf Coast.
1934	Severe dust storms sweep across the Great Plains in the U.S., destroying homes and crops.
1954	Hurricane Carol is the first hurricane whose name is later retired because of the hurricane's destructiveness.
1973	The Saffir-Simpson Hurricane Scale is first used to classify hurricanes based on their sustained wind speeds.
1988	Severe heat and weather patterns prompt the UN to form the IPCC.
2005	Hurricane Katrina strikes the Gulf Coast, killing 1,836 people and flooding much of New Orleans.
2012	Superstorm Sandy makes landfall in New Jersey and causes massive destruction and a 10-day blackout in the New York metropolitan area.
2013	Typhoon Haiyan strikes the Philippines with 195-mile-per-hour (314 km) winds, killing more than 7,000 people.
2015	Most countries sign the UNFCCC, agreeing to limit global warming.
2017	Hurricane Maria knocks out power for more than 3 million people in Puerto Rico and is responsible for nearly 3,000 deaths.
2018	Wildfires destroy forests and communities in both northern and southern California.

carbon monoxide—a colorless, odorless gas that can be deadly if too much is breathed in

droughts—long periods of dry weather in which crops fail and farmland dries up

fossil fuels—natural fuels such as coal, oil, or gas, formed in the geological past from the remains of living organisms; burning fossil fuels gives off carbon dioxide, which may contribute to global warming

glaciers—large masses of ice formed over a long period of time from the packing and freezing of snow

green energy—energy that comes from natural, renewable sources such as sunlight, wind, rushing water, and plants

hailstorms—thunderstorms in which pellets of frozen rain (hail) reach the ground

hurricane level—storm strength in which wind speeds exceed 74 miles (119 km) per hour

industrialization—a period in which people began to use machines powered by fossil fuel sources to do work

landfall—when a tropical storm leaves the ocean and encounters land

Renaissance—the historical period in Europe between the 14th and 17th centuries when there was a renewed interest in art, literature, and science

sea level—the level of the sea's surface in relation to shorelines

solar panels—devices designed to absorb the sun's rays to generate electricity or heat

Spanish Armada—a fleet of warships sent by Spain to attack England in 1588

storm surge—a rising of the sea, pushed by air pressure changes, tides, and strong winds; it often causes flooding

tsunamis—high, powerful sea waves, often caused by earthquakes, that can cause great damage and drown many people when they come ashore

water vapor—the gaseous form of water in the air

Cerveny, Randy. *Freaks of the Storm: The World's Strangest True Weather Stories.* New York: Thunder's Mouth Press, 2006.

Climate Central. *Global Weirdness: Severe Storms, Deadly Heat Waves, Relentless Drought, Rising Seas, and the Weather of the Future.* New York: Pantheon Books, 2012.

Cunningham, Anne C., and Kenneth Green. *Climate Change: A Threat to All Life on Earth.* New York: Enslow, 2016.

Encyclopedia Britannica. *Weather and Climate.* Chicago: Encyclopedia Britannica, 2008.

Intergovernmental Panel on *Climate Change.* "Special Report: Global Warming of 1.5 °C." *https://www.ipcc.ch/sr15/.*

Kostigen, Thomas M. *Extreme Weather.* Washington, D.C.: National Geographic, 2014.

Schneider, Bonnie. *Extreme Weather.* New York: Palgrave Macmillan, 2012.

Sobel, Adam. *Storm Surge: Hurricane Sandy, Our Changing Climate, and Extreme Weather of the Past and Future.* New York: HarperCollins, 2014.

National Oceanic and Atmospheric Administration
https://www.noaa.gov/
Learn about the conditions of the oceans, major waterways, and the atmosphere.

NASA: Global Climate Change
https://climate.nasa.gov
This site provides up-to-date articles and resources on climate change.

Note: Every effort has been made to ensure that the websites listed above are suitable for children, that they have educational value, and that they contain no inappropriate material. However, because of the nature of the Internet, it is impossible to guarantee that these sites will remain active indefinitely or that their contents will not be altered.